Contents

"To harm other people is understandable in our culture but to willingly harm yourself is thought of as perverted."

Introduction

Self-harm is a very common problem, and many people are struggling to deal with it. Perhaps you feel or have felt the need to harm yourself. Perhaps you have been self-harming for some time. Or maybe you have a friend, brother or sister or a son or daughter who is self-harming, or someone you teach or work with is doing it and you need to know more.

This booklet is for anyone who wants to understand self-harm among young people - why it happens, how to deal with it, and how to recover from what can become a very destructive cycle.

Self-harm can be difficult to understand – both for those who do it and also for those who care about them. It is also a subject that has not received much attention up until now, and is still treated as 'taboo' by many. But it happens a lot more than people think.

The most important thing to understand is that you can recover from the pattern of self-harm, and from feeling the urge to harm yourself.

"Don't get me wrong, not in a heartbeat do I think that self-harm is a good or positive thing, or anything besides a heart-breaking desperate act that saddens me every time I hear about it. But there's a reason why people do it."

Understanding self-harm

Many find it almost impossible to understand why young people harm themselves, and how it could possibly help them to feel better. By deliberately hurting their bodies, young people often say they can change their state of mind so that they can cope better with 'other' pain they are feeling. They may be using physical pain as a way of distracting themselves from emotional pain. Others are conscious of a sense of release. For some, especially those who feel emotionally scarred, it may be a way to 'wake up' in situations where they are so numb they can't feel anything. Overall, self-harm is a way of dealing with intense emotional pain.

Self-harm has a huge impact on the day-to-day life of those who do it. They will often try hard to keep what they're doing secret, and to hide their scars and bruises. But the burden of guilt and secrecy is difficult to carry. It can affect everything from what they wear to the kinds of sports and physical activities they take part in, as well as close physical relationships with others, including sexual relationships.

Ultimately, because young people who do it are all too aware of the stigma of self-harm, it can affect their relationships with friends and family and their sense of self-worth. Young people start self-harming to cope with their problems and feelings, but it very soon creates other serious problems. It can set up an addictive pattern of behaviour, from which it can be very hard to break free.

What is self-harm?

The phrase 'self-harm' is used to describe a range of things that people do to themselves in a deliberate and usually hidden way. It can involve:

- cutting
- burning
- scalding
- banging or scratching one's own body
- breaking bones
- hair pulling
- swallowing poisonous substances or objects

> "I felt a warm sense of relief, as though all the bad things about me were flowing out of me and it made me feel alive, real."

Who does it?

Research shows that 1 in 15 young people in Britain have harmed themselves. Another way of looking at it is that there are probably two young people in every secondary school classroom who have done it at some time. This means it's a very common problem.

Most young people who harm themselves are aged between 11 and 25. The age at which most people start is 12, but some children as young as 7 have been known to do it.

There is no such thing as a 'typical' young person who self-harms. About four times as many girls as boys do it. But it is also a serious problem among young men. Because they are more likely to do things like hitting themselves or breaking their own bones it can look as if they have had an accident, a fight or have been attacked.

Some very young children self-harm, and some adults too. Groups of people who are more vulnerable to self-harm than others include:

- young people in residential settings like the armed forces, prison, sheltered housing or hostels and boarding schools
- lesbian, gay, bisexual and transgender young people
- young Asian women
- young people with learning disabilities

Why do young people self-harm?

As one young person put it, many people self-harm to 'get out the hurt, anger and pain' caused by pressures in their lives. They harm themselves because they don't know what else to do and because they don't have, or don't feel they have, any other options.

For some young people, self-harm gives temporary relief and a sense of control over their lives. But it brings its own very serious problems.

When asked about the issues that led them to self-harm, young people most often said it was linked with:

• Being bullied at school

• Stress and worry about school work and exams

• Feeling isolated

• Not getting on with parents or other family members

• Parents getting divorced

• Bereavement

• Unwanted pregnancy

• Experience of abuse earlier in childhood

• Current abuse – physical, sexual or verbal

• The self-harm or suicide of someone close to them

• Problems to do with sexuality

• Problems to do with race, culture or religion

• Low self-esteem

• Feelings of rejection socially or within their families

If you are being abused, it is vital that you get help. Please see the 'Where can I get further help and information?' section at the end of this booklet.

"Some people do it for attention... that doesn't mean they should be ignored. There are plenty of ways to get attention, why cause yourself pain? And if someone's crying for help, you should give them it, not stand there and judge the way they're asking for it."

Myths and stereotypes

There are lots of these attached to self-harm. This isn't surprising – myths and misunderstandings often arise when a problem is, like self-harm, poorly understood.

Negative stereotypes can be powerful. They need to be challenged because they stop young people from coming forward for help. They also mean that professionals, family and friends are much more likely to react in a hostile way to young people who self-harm.

Some of the most common stereotypes are that self-harm is about 'attention seeking'. Most self-harm is actually done in secret, for a long time and it can be very hard for young people to find enough courage to ask for help.

Self-harm is sometimes seen as a group activity – especially when young people are 'goths'. But it's very rarely a group activity. Young people told the Inquiry that they couldn't say how many people they knew who self-harmed, because no one wants to talk about it. The Inquiry could find no evidence to support the belief that this behaviour may be part of a particular youth sub-culture.

Is self-harm linked to suicide?

It is often the belief that self-harm is closely linked to suicide that frightens people most. But the vast majority of young people who self-harm are not trying to kill themselves – they are trying to cope with difficult feelings and circumstances – for many it is a way of staying alive. Many people who commit suicide have self-harmed in the past, and this is one of the many reasons that self-harm must be taken very seriously.

How do people self-harm?

As shown earlier, there are lots of ways of self-harming. The most common is cutting yourself.

People who self-harm tend to go to great lengths to keep it secret. Young people can be hurting themselves over long periods of time without ever telling friends or family. They hardly ever seek medical attention or support.

Almost all self-harm is done in private, and on parts of the body that are not visible to others.

"People often link self-harm to suicide but for me it was something very different; it was my alternative to suicide; my way of coping even though sometimes I wished that my world would end!"

How does it start?

Many young people say that when they first harm themselves they believe it is a 'one-off' and that they won't do it again. But it doesn't solve the problems they are trying to cope with, and their difficult feelings soon come back again, leading them into a cycle of harming themselves to try to cope.

Some young people have told us that they started to self-harm by accident – when they injured themselves accidentally and then started to cause themselves injuries on purpose to create the same feelings again.

Is it really addictive?

It is habit-forming, and some people believe you can become physically addicted to self-harm. There is evidence to show that chemicals, called 'endogenous opioids' are released when the body is injured in any way. They are pleasurable and can make you less sensitive to pain. However, self-harm is not simply about chasing physical pleasure or relief through artificially stimulating a 'natural' reaction – it has to be understood for what it means to the young person who does it. Often it is a way of coping or distracting yourself, that is habit-forming. In other words, young people get used to it, and come to rely on it.

How do young people feel about harming themselves?

Young people who self-harm usually feel very guilty and ashamed of what they do, and do not want to talk about it. The stigma associated with self-harm is unhelpful, and stops people getting the support and information they need to find better and more helpful ways of coping.

What are the signs that someone is self-harming?

It is very difficult to tell whether someone is self-harming. One sign might be that they insist on covering up their bodies – even when it is warm. They may avoid activities that involve showing themselves – such as swimming or games. Secretive behaviour, and wanting to be alone lots can also be a sign.

Many of the usual signs of emotional distress – becoming withdrawn, quiet, appearing 'washed out' and lacking energy, can also be signs that someone is self-harming.

"I feel a lot more confident. I've learned to be more open about my feelings and been able to move on. I felt that, without them knowing, I was being held back. I've been able to come out of myself and explain what I do, and make sense of it, not keep having to lie and cover up what I did. I no longer feel ashamed as I know people are supporting me."

Talking about self-harm

Why do people self-harm in secret? Why don't they ask for help?

When we asked young people who have self-harmed what stopped them from seeking help, they often said that at first they thought the behaviour was a 'one off', and it was only after a few times that they found they couldn't stop.

But one of the biggest fears young people told us about, and the biggest obstacle to getting help, was the fear that self-harm, the only coping strategy that had been keeping them going, might be taken away from them.

They also said that they thought they could cope on their own, or that they were planning to sort things out and didn't need any help.

Many young people were worried about what others would think of them, when they found out they were hurting themselves intentionally. They were also worried that they would not be taken seriously. Many feared that no one would understand why they had done it, or would be able to help them. Girls were particularly sensitive about being labelled or dismissed as being an 'attention seeker' or 'stupid' if they asked for help.

Most young people felt that they would not self-harm again, and they wanted to put the fact that they had done it to the back of their minds. Boys in particular felt that the situation and their injuries were not serious enough to ask for help. Very few young people understood at the beginning that things might change for the worse again, and that they could come to depend on harming themselves to cope with their lives.

Many young people said they did not have anyone they felt they could talk to apart, sometimes, from close friends. They certainly didn't know how to contact support services. Some were worried that if they were open about their self-harm, this could affect their choices for the future: they were worried they wouldn't be able to work in professions such as teaching, nursing, or childcare because of perceptions that people who self-harm are 'dangerous' and should not be allowed to work with children.

Young people also told us they were worried that their secret would become 'public property' and that they would lose control over the situation and who knew about it, once they told someone else.

Should I tell someone that I am harming myself?

Yes, because this is often the first step to getting out of the cycle.

It isn't always simple or easy, and could be one of the most difficult – but most important things you do. Young people have told us that the reaction they got when they first told someone about their self-harm was very important in deciding whether or not they looked for and got further help.

While some young people have experienced negative attitudes when they have told someone, it is possible to get good support from people who understand self harm, or who care about you and your feelings, not just the behaviour itself.

If you are worried about the person you tell sharing the information with others, you can choose to tell a health professional like a doctor or a nurse to start with, or a counsellor. You can also telephone a helpline (see 'where to get help' section). These people have a duty to keep it to themselves while you get used to the idea of telling others. They can offer you help and advice while you prepare.

Unfortunately, some young people told us that they felt forced into discussing their self-harm, for example by teachers or health professionals who had guessed what was going on. Some young people felt very distressed by the idea that these workers would tell others – like fellow teachers or their parents. If this happens to you, you could try explaining that self-harm is a coping mechanism and not the same as suicidal behaviour.

You can ask them what will happen next, once you have told them, and who else they plan to tell or involve. You can ask them not to tell particular people. You can even ask them not to tell anyone at all, although this can be very difficult for the other person, and it can mean you do not get all of the help and support that you need.

"The one thing that always helps if I'm feeling really bad is to be around someone that I trust. I may look bad and not be very talkative – but just being around someone who doesn't question my odd behaviour and lets me be around them without talking or expectations helps."

What is the best way to tell someone that I have harmed myself?

It can be a very worrying decision, and it can be hard to decide who to tell and how to tell them. Telling someone about your self-harm shows strength and courage. But it can often be a huge relief to be able to let go of such a secret, or at least share it.

The most important thing of all is that you feel comfortable with who you decide to tell, what you tell them, when and where. Don't feel pressured into answering questions or saying more than you want to. You can set the pace. Remember, if you want to tell a professional or family member, you can take a friend with you to support you.

There are many ways of telling people and there are no rules about how it should be done. You can speak to someone, write to or email them, or even just show them your injuries or scars and let that pave the way to talking about it. If you tell someone in writing, think about taking some time to talk to them afterwards, as well.

It is very important, if you can, to try to focus on the feelings or situation that led you to start harming yourself, rather than on the behaviour itself. This can help people feel less bewildered about why you might be doing it.

Revealing self-harm to someone can bring out a wide range of feelings in them, both positive and negative. The person you tell may need some time to get used to what you have told them and think about their response, so try to give this to them. They may well be able to respond more positively after some time has passed and they have had the chance to think over what you have said. It can be helpful to them to know why you are telling them – whether you just want to let go of a secret you have carried on your own, or you would like their help or advice.

As hard as telling someone may be for you, it may also be very hard for the person you choose to tell – especially if it is someone close to you. They may need to get support for themselves, both before and after talking about it with you.

Try to be prepared for the fact that sometimes your situation can feel worse immediately after telling someone. But once you are over this hurdle, there is usually support available to help you recover – even if the support is through friends or family.

Who can I tell?

A major factor in how the person you tell responds will be the kind of relationship they have with you, and how well they know you. A parent who might feel they are very close to you may be more shocked, for example, than a nurse.

Most people (no matter who they are, a friend, a parent, a teacher or a professional) don't really understand self-harm, and it's hard to predict how someone will react when you tell them. Try to keep in mind that they may have a range of feelings, and one of them will most likely be shock.

Young people have told us that the people they have been able to talk to included:

• Friends – young people said they were far more likely to talk it over with friends their own age than anyone else

• Family members

• Someone at school but not necessarily a teacher you know well

• Telephone help lines were also mentioned

• Internet support: not many people had looked for help on the internet, but there are some useful sources online.

• A doctor or nurse

Some young people have said that the reaction they got when talking to health workers was unhelpful. In this case you can always seek further help. Many GPs and nurses will be sympathetic, and know how to help and no-one should be put off from seeking help because of negative attitudes.

"Many **people** stop **hurting themselves when the time** is right for **them. Everyone is different and** if they **feel the** need to **self-harm** at the moment, they shouldn't **feel** guilty about it - it is a way of surviving, and doing it now does NOT mean that they **will** need to do it forever. It is a **huge** step towards stopping **when** they **begin** to talk about it, **because** it means that **they** are starting to think about **what might take** its place eventually."

What if someone tells me they are self-harming?

The reaction a young person receives when they disclose their self-harm has a major impact on whether they go on to get help and recover. What young people who self-harm need is understanding, care and concern for their injuries, time and support as well as encouragement to talk about the underlying feelings or situations that have led them to harm themselves. Getting angry, shouting, or accusing them is likely to aggravate the situation.

Young people who have self-harmed want responses that are non-judgemental, caring and respectful. It's very important to see the person, and the reasons they have harmed themselves, and not just to focus on the harm itself. It's also important to allow the young person to take the discussion at their own pace.

Most importantly, you should try to hear about self-harm without panic, revulsion or condemnation. This can be hard as it's difficult to understand, but remember, it is quite common, and it's usually used as a way of coping by young people.

If you are a friend of the person who is self-harming, you might have some of the same reactions that a parent would – disbelief, fear for your friend, worry about what to do for the best. The person may tell you but want you to keep it a secret. This can leave you feeling distressed and isolated, with no-one to talk to yourself.

Working out what to do, or trying to decide how much danger your friend is in, is not easy. It may be useful to try one of the places to go for further help that is listed in this booklet. It may also be helpful, if you are a young person, to find someone older that you trust and believe you can confide in.

Occasionally, someone may reveal to you that they have harmed themselves immediately after they have injured themselves – perhaps more than they meant to. They may be worried that they have done lasting damage. If this happens it is best to see that their injuries are attended to and they have time to recover from any physical trauma before exploring the reasons behind it.

What if I discover my son or daughter or someone I care for is self-harming?

Try to be accepting and open-minded. Let the person know you are there for them, and reassure them that they are loved. Assure them that it's okay to talk about their need to self-harm, and reassure them that they have your support even if you don't understand why they are doing it or what they are going through.

Offer to lend a hand in getting them professional help; from a GP, counsellor, therapist, or community psychiatric nurse. But try to avoid taking control-many people who self-harm feel it is an important way of having some control over their lives. Try to not to take it too personally if your son or daughter cannot talk to you because you are too close.

Avoid giving ultimatums; for example, 'stop or else…' as they rarely work, and may well drive the behaviour underground, and you might not get any further chances to discuss the topic and really deal with it. Self-harm can be very addictive, and if a person feels the need to do it, they will normally find a way. It is important that the decision to stop comes from the person who is self-harming.

Find out more. There are a growing number of useful books on the topic of self-harm, as well as some informative websites. Educating yourself on the subject can go a long way towards helping you be understanding and supportive.

Try to sort out your own feelings. Be honest with yourself about how your daughter or son's self-harm is affecting you. It's not unusual to feel hurt, devastated, shocked, angry, sad, frightened, guilty, responsible, hopeless, or powerless. It's not easy knowing that a loved one is hurting him or herself, and it might be worth considering seeing a counsellor or therapist for yourself if you are struggling to cope with strong emotions or feel in need of support.

Remember, finding out that someone is self-harming is a real opportunity to help them deal with many other problems they are having.

"It dawned on me that continually harming myself was not allowing me to grow; it was just proving that I was still here and I could feel. But it wasn't letting me push things forward, and unless I stopped doing that I would be in the same wretched situation forever."

Getting help

What sort of help is available for young people who self-harm?

Most young people who have found help say that having someone to listen to them and help them to work on solutions to their problems and stresses is the most helpful thing of all. This is why counselling or another type of talking therapy is useful. Ask your doctor to refer you to a counsellor or psychotherapist.

Over-18's who talk to health professionals about their self-harm find that some of them are very keen to prescribe drugs such as anti-depressants. You may or may not want to try these as part of your recovery plan.

There may also be self-help groups that you can contact, where you can meet other people who have been through similar experiences to you. This can be very helpful. See page 27 for further information.

How can I stop harming myself?

Most importantly, try to focus on the feelings that seem to lead you to self-harm, and what is causing them. You may need the help of friends, family, a counsellor or psychotherapist, or a doctor or nurse. This is why asking for help is so important. Earlier on in this booklet you will find lots of information about telling someone that you are harming yourself. This is often the first step towards getting the help you need.

By finding out what makes you happy, sad, angry, isolated, vulnerable or strong, you can start developing other ways of dealing with these situations and feelings. It may help just to stop and give yourself time to think them through. If you feel the need to harm yourself, give yourself a goal of getting through the next ten minutes without doing so, and try to focus on what is making you feel that way.

If you don't feel you can stop straight away, start finding other things that help you to deal with your moods and feelings. This should help you to harm yourself less and less frequently after a while – and the more effort you put in, the less strong the need to harm yourself will become.

One of the most useful things that other young people have done is to learn 'distraction methods'. These are special ways of finding a release without doing yourself any real damage. Some of the most popular, tried and tested ways of distracting yourself follow.

What if I think someone is self-harming but they won't talk about it?

This can be very difficult. It is often best to discuss how the person is feeling and explain that you have noticed changes in their behaviour, rather than asking straight out. Self-harm can be a difficult subject to introduce, so take it slowly.

How do I stop someone from self-harming?

It may be very difficult if someone you care about is self-harming, but trying to force them to stop doesn't work. It is very clear that self-harm in many cases is a pattern of behaviour that may have gone on for a long time, and most young people would find it virtually impossible to give up overnight, even if they wanted to. Feeling in control is something that young people who self-harm say is very important to them. The good news is that being able to take control is one of the most important factors in the ability to recover from a pattern of self-harm, too. It is very important that the decision to stop comes from the person who is self-harming.

For many young people stopping or reducing their self-harm is a long and slow process. Young people need the opportunity to build up their coping skills gradually, and may go on harming themselves for some time.

It can take time for young people to reach the point where they can start to give up. In the meantime, learning how to cause themselves the least possible damage can be crucial, and the first step in their journey to learning other ways to deal with difficult feelings. This is called 'harm reduction' and you can find out more about this from other organisations like Siari (see page 27 for details).

For most of the young people we spoke to, the recovery process began with tackling the underlying problems that were causing their self-harm. This sometimes involved counselling, sharing their problems, or tackling bullies. Helping a young person to tackle their underlying problems is something you can very usefully do.

They also broke the habit by learning new coping strategies or using 'distraction techniques' (see next section) when they felt the urge to hurt themselves. Different people need different distraction methods, and may need different things for different moods or situations. Finding what is most helpful takes time, but young people who have persisted with it emphasise that trial and error will find something that works.

Substitutes for self-harm

Young people have shared their most successful ones with us, and these are:

- using a red felt tip pen to mark where you might usually cut
- hitting a punch bag to vent anger and frustration
- hitting pillows or cushions, or having a good scream into a pillow or cushion
- rubbing ice across your skin where you might usually cut, or holding an ice-cube in the crook of your arm or leg
- getting outdoors and having a fast walk
- all other forms of exercise – these are really good at changing your mood and releasing adrenaline
- making lots of noise, either with a musical instrument or just banging on pots and pans
- writing negative feelings on a piece of paper and then ripping it up
- keeping a journal
- scribbling on a large piece of paper with a red crayon or pen
- putting elastic bands on wrists, arms or legs and flicking them instead of cutting or hitting
- calling and talking to a friend (not necessarily about self-harm)
- collage or artwork – doing something creative
- going online and looking at self-help websites

"I've tried so many distraction techniques - from holding an ice-cube, elastic band flicking on the wrist, writing down my thoughts, hitting a pillow, listening to music, writing down pros and cons. But the most helpful to my recovery was the five minutes rule, where if you feel like you want to self-harm you wait for five minutes before you do, then see if you can go another five minutes, and so on till eventually the urge is over."

How I do recover from feeling the need to self-harm?

Some of the information in the section about how to stop self-harming covers dealing with the feelings that make you want to do it. This is vitally important if you want to break the habit in the long term.

It's important to remember that you won't always feel the way you do now. Some of the problems that are causing you to self-harm will go away – sometimes with and sometimes without your help.

Young people who have recovered from needing to self-harm say that changes over time, for example moving home, changing schools, finishing exams, going to university, changing jobs or changed financial circumstances have helped them to recover. Once one or two of the original factors (such as their family situation, or bullying at school) were removed, they felt they didn't have to use self-harm as a coping strategy. Sometimes, just the sense of things 'moving on' was enough to help them stop.

Other ways to help yourself are to listen to the many other young people who have moved on in their lives, and are feeling strong and happy. Many of their voices are present in this booklet in the form of quotes. And you will find many others on the websites of organisations set up to help people in your position. You may want to get together with other young people going through similar things to you – perhaps using self-help groups or the Internet.

Accept help, wherever and whenever you can get it. For young people too used to carrying burdens on their own, it can be harder to receive than to give. Part of your recovery may involve trusting people enough to let them help you. When the time is right, you may be able to help others in your turn

Take time – you don't have to recover overnight. It can be a slow process. Don't expect miracles from yourself or from anyone else. Learn how to care for yourself.

Looking after yourself - for good

It's important to look after your mental health, always. Following are some of the best ways of doing it.

- Eat well. A healthy, and balanced diet is vital for your mental well-being. A diet rich in carbohydrates is thought to increase levels of serotonin in the brain, which is thought to improve mood. Mood swings, depression, anxiety and restlessness – which can be related to diet – are often said by young people to be triggers for their self-harm. Caffeine can produce a temporary 'high', but in the long term it can lead to sleeping problems, and an over stimulated nervous system, which raises anxiety levels (which in turn is linked to depression). To find out more visit www.mentalhealth.org.uk

- Avoid alcohol, or drink sensibly. Alcohol can leave you feeling depressed or anxious, and can lower your inhibitions physically, which can lead you back to harming yourself.

- Take lots of exercise. It's one of the best ways to look after your mental health – and a quick burst of exercise can even help you change your mood almost instantly. Frequent exercise can help young people who self-harm reduce anxiety, decrease depression, improve mood, think better and can actually improve their sense of self worth. It can help you look and feel better, which is vital for people who have low self esteem and worry about their appearance. Exercise is now used to treat mental health problems like depression – it's something you can do for ever – and it doesn't have the stigma that some people associate with counselling or therapy or antidepressants.

- Do something you're good at. This is one of the best ways of looking after your mental health. Perhaps you can do something creative, a sport or a hobby. Perhaps you're good at looking after other people.

- Stay in touch. Friends are important. Keeping up with old friends and making new friends can keep you mentally and emotionally well. Try joining a new book club or sports or other activity group.

- Ask for help – whenever and however you need it. Identify the people who can help you, who you trust. These people make up your most important support network, and can help you deal with crises and problems in the future without you turning back to self-harm.

- Don't drive yourself too hard. Many young people who self-harm are high-achievers, and sometimes they put themselves under too much pressure. Sometimes it's OK for your work or your performance to be "good enough".

Where can I get further help and information?

Self-help and support groups are very popular with young people who self-harm as they enable them to explore their feelings, why they do it, and how they cope. These groups help young people to feel less isolated, find friendships and they offer a safe place to talk openly and honestly without fearing the responses they might get. These groups may or may not be available, depending on where you live. To find out more, it is worth asking your doctor or nurse, or visiting your nearest Citizens Advice Bureau. You may also find them by searching on the Internet.

Websites and internet forums have become increasingly popular with young people as a way to access information and support for a range of different issues including self-harm. Many young people – especially young men, who tend not to engage in traditional face-to-face services – find this useful. It is important that young people know where to get good information. Some websites that have been recommended to us by young people include:

- www.siari.co.uk
- www.youthnet.org
- www.lifesigns.org.uk
- www.childline.org.uk
- www.samaritans.org.uk
- www.selfharm.org.uk

Some telephone helplines offer specialist advice on self-harm, others operate only as a 'friendly listening ear' – something many young people have said they value, particularly when they feel they have no-one else that they can turn to. Again, it's important that information about reputable phone lines is widely available to young people. Helpful telephone numbers include:

- ChildLine – 0800 1111
- Samaritans – 08457 90 90 90
- Parentline Plus – 0808 800 2222
- NSPCC – 0808 800 5000

There are now more counselling services available – some through special organisations set up to help people who self-harm. Ask your doctor to refer you to a counsellor, contact your local council, or visit your nearest Citizens Advice Bureau to find out what counselling services are available near you.

Appendix

The National Inquiry into self-harm and its recommendations

The Inquiry found that lots more needs to be done to help young people who self-harm, or who may turn to it in the future. If you would like further information, the Inquiry website will point you in the right direction.

The Inquiry had many findings and recommendations, mostly for central Government departments and various groups of professionals. They included:

- A call for Government to pay more attention to the issue of self-harm, because it affects so many young people's lives

- An expressed need for research to find out which young people self-harm, including understanding how ethnicity, gender, and sexuality affect self-harm

- A need for more research to find out why certain environments like closed residential settings seem to be more likely to trigger self-harm, and what can be done to change these environments

- A call for Government to run a national awareness campaign, so that people can better understand why young people self-harm

- More work in schools including whole-school approaches, to see how they work to prevent self-harm and help young people who are doing it

- Professionals, such as teachers, youth workers, nurses and GPs need training and support in how to deal with young people who self-harm